Math in Focus

Singapore Math®
by Marshall Cavendish

Extra Practice and Homework

Program Consultant
Dr. Fong Ho Kheong

Author
Chelvi Ramakrishnan

Marshall Cavendish Education

U.S. Distributor

Houghton Mifflin Harcourt.
The Learning Company™

Grade 4B

© 2020 Marshall Cavendish Education Pte Ltd

Published by Marshall Cavendish Education
Times Centre, 1 New Industrial Road, Singapore 536196
Customer Service Hotline: (65) 6213 9688
US Office Tel: (1-914) 332 8888 | Fax: (1-914) 332 8882
E-mail: cs@mceducation.com
Website: www.mceducation.com

Distributed by
Houghton Mifflin Harcourt
125 High Street
Boston, MA 02110
Tel: 617-351-5000
Website: www.hmhco.com/programs/math-in-focus

First published 2020

ISBN 978-0-358-10305-9

Printed in Singapore

3 4 5 6 7 8 9   1401   26 25 24 23 22 21
4500817404   B C D E F

The cover image shows an Angolan giraffe.
Giraffes can be found in many African countries, out on the open plains. A giraffe's long neck allows it to reach up high to feed on new leaf shoots at the top of trees. Giraffes live in herds and can run fast to get away from lions and other predators. They sleep for about four hours a day.

Contents

Chapter 5   **Conversion of Measurements**

School-to-Home Connections		1
Activity 1	Length in Customary Units	3
Activity 2	Weight and Volume in Customary Units	5
Activity 3	Real-World Problems: Customary Units of Measure	9
Activity 4	Length in Metric Units	13
Activity 5	Mass and Volume in Metric Units	17
Activity 6	Real-World Problems: Metric Units of Measure	21
Activity 7	Time	25
Math Journal		31
Put on Your Thinking Cap!		32

Chapter 6   **Area and Perimeter**

School-to-Home Connections		33
Activity 1	Area and Unknown Sides	35
Activity 2	Composite Figures	43
Activity 3	Real-World Problems: Area and Perimeter	47
Math Journal		53
Put on Your Thinking Cap!		54

Chapter 7   **Angles and Line Segments**

School-to-Home Connections		55
Activity 1	Understanding and Measuring Angles	57
Activity 2	Drawing Angles to 180°	59
Activity 3	Turns and Angle Measures	63
Activity 4	Finding Unknown Angles	65
Activity 5	Drawing Perpendicular and Parallel Line Segments	67
Math Journal		71
Put on Your Thinking Cap!		72

Chapter 8   **Polygons and Symmetry**

School-to-Home Connections		**73**
Activity 1	Classifying Triangles	**75**
Activity 2	Classifying Polygons	**77**
Activity 3	Symmetric Shapes and Lines of Symmetry	**79**
Activity 4	Making Symmetric Shapes and Patterns	**83**
Math Journal		**85**
Put on Your Thinking Cap!		**86**

Chapter 9   **Tables and Line Graphs**

School-to-Home Connections		**87**
Activity 1	Making and Interpreting a Table	**89**
Activity 2	Using a Table	**93**
Activity 3	Line Graphs	**95**
Math Journal		**97**
Put on Your Thinking Cap!		**98**

© 2020 Marshall Cavendish Education Pte Ltd

Preface

Welcome!

Math in Focus®: Singapore Math® *Extra Practice and Homework* is written to be used with the **Math in Focus®**: Singapore Math® *Student Edition*, to support your learning.

This book provides activities and problems that closely follow what you have learned in the Student Edition.

- In **Activities**, you practice the concepts and skills you learned in the Student Edition, so that you can master the concepts and build your confidence.

- In **MATH JOURNAL**, you reflect on your thinking when you write down your thoughts about the math concepts you learned.

- In **PUT ON YOUR THINKING CAP!**, you develop your problem-solving and critical thinking skills, and challenge yourself to apply concepts in different ways.

This book also includes **SCHOOL-to-HOME CONNECTIONS**. Each family letter summarizes the learning objectives and the key mathematical vocabulary you are using. The letter also includes one or more activities that your family can do with you to support your learning further.

BLANK

SCHOOL-to-HOME
CONNECTIONS

Conversion of Measurements

Dear Family,

In this chapter, your child will learn about converting metric and customary measures of length, mass, weight, and volume, and units of time. Skills your child will practice include:

- measuring, estimating, and converting metric and customary units of length
- measuring, estimating, and converting metric units of mass and customary units of weight
- measuring, estimating, and converting metric and customary units of volume
- measuring time in seconds
- converting units of time
- solving real-world problems involving metric and customary units of measure and time

Math Practice

At the end of this chapter, you may want to carry out these activities with your child. These activities will help your child practice converting measurements.

Activity 1

- Have your child list some items in the pantry and record the measurement of each item found in the label.
- Then, get him or her to convert each measurement to the nearest unit of measurement, for example, kilograms to grams, pounds to ounces, and liters to milliliters.

Activity 2

- Give your child a map of your town, city, or country. Guide your child to the distances indicated from one point to another on the map, such as, from the town center to the park or from your child's school to home.
- Then, get him or her to convert each measurement to the nearest unit of measurement.

Math Talk

Help your child make conversions using **metric** and **customary** units of measurement.

Customary units of length
foot (ft), inch (in.), yard (yd), mile (mi)
1 ft = 12 in.
1 yd = 3 ft
1 mi = 1,760 yd

Customary units of weight
pound (lb), ounce (oz), ton (T)
1 lb = 16 oz
1 T = 2,000 lb

Customary units of volume
1 pint = 2 cups
1 quart = 2 pints
1 gallon = 4 quarts

Metric units of length
meter (m), centimeter (cm), kilometer (km)
1 m = 100 cm
1 km = 1,000 m

Metric units of mass
kilogram (kg), gram (g)
1 kg = 1,000 g

Metric units of volume
liter (L), milliliter (mL)
1 L = 1,000 mL

Units of time
hour (h), minute (min), seconds (sec)
1 min = 60 sec
1 h = 60 min

BLANK

Name: _____ Date: _____

Activity 1   Length in Customary Units

Choose the unit that you would use to measure each object. Use "inch," "foot," "yard," or "mile."

1 the length of a television set _____

2 the length of a wall _____

3 the length of a basketball court _____

4 the distance between two cities _____

Underline the best estimate of each object.

5 The length of a stapler is about 3 (inches / feet / yards / miles).

6 A shrub is about 4 (inches / feet / yards / miles) high.

7 A car took 3 hours to travel 100 (inches / feet / yards / miles).

Circle the object that is about 1 inch long.

8

Fill in each blank.

9 A door is 3 feet wide. Express the width in inches.

The width of the door is _____ inches.

10 A soccer field is 52 yards wide. Express the width in feet.

The width of the soccer field is _____ feet.

Solve. Show your work.

11 Riley ran 2 miles on a particular day. Owen ran 2,000 yards on the same day. Who ran a longer distance?

12 Julia walked 380 feet from her home to her school. Her classmate Santino walked 120 yards from his home to school. Who walked a shorter distance?

Name: _____   Date: _____

Activity 2   Weight and Volume in Customary Units

Fill in each blank.

1

The weight of the crabs is
about _____ pounds.

2

The weight of the packet of
flour is about _____ pounds.

Choose the unit that you would use to measure each object. Use "ounce," "pound," or "ton."

3 the weight of a pen   _____

4 the weight of a doll   _____

5 the weight of an airplane   _____

Underline the best estimate of each object.

6 The volume of a bottle of perfume is about 1.7 (fluid ounces / cups / pints / quarts / gallons).

7 About 3 (fluid ounces / cups / pints / quarts / gallons) of flour are needed to bake a cake.

8 The volume of a carton of milk is about 1 (fluid ounce / cup / pint / quart / gallon).

9 A pail can hold about 10 (fluid ounces / cups / pints / quarts / gallons) of liquid.

10 The volume of a tin of peanut oil is about 3 (fluid ounces / cups / pints / quarts / gallons).

Fill in each blank.

11 12 lb = _____ oz

12 4 T = _____ oz

13 8 c = _____ fl oz

14 15 pt = _____ c

15 17 pt = _____ fl oz

16 23 qt = _____ pt

17 29 qt = _____ c

18 35 qt = _____ c

19 7 gal = _____ pt

20 24 gal = _____ c

Compare each pair of volumes. Write >, <, or =.

21 9 oz ◯ 4 lb

22 8,500 lb ◯ 6 T

23 3 c ◯ 3 pt

24 15 pt ◯ 13 c

25 18 pt ◯ 300 fl oz

26 16 qt ◯ 8 pt

27 500 fl oz ◯ 25 pt

28 12 c ◯ 48 qt

29 3 gal ◯ 24 pt

30 7 gal ◯ 19 qt

31 98 c ◯ 14 gal

32 21 c ◯ 168 fl oz

Solve. Show your work.

33 There are 4 cups of orange juice in a pitcher. If we add 9 fluid ounces of lemon juice, what is the volume of the mixture?

34 A local hospital conducted a blood drive and collected a total of 100 pints of blood from donors. The hospital was hoping to collect 10 gallons of blood from the drive. Did the hospital meet its goal? How much more or less blood did the hospital collect?

Name: _____ Date: _____

Chapter 5

Extra Practice and Homework
Conversion of Measurements

Activity 3   Real-World Problems: Customary Units of Measure

Solve. Show your work.

1   Ms. Jones uses 3 cups of milk and Ms. Smith uses 19 fluid ounces of milk to make some waffles.
Who uses more milk?

2   Ryan collected 87 pints of rainwater, and Lucia collected 7 gallons of rainwater to water their gardens. Who collected more rainwater?

3 A roll of tape is 30 feet long. A box contains 375 rolls of tape. How many yards of tape are there in all?

4 A parking spot is 8 feet wide. A parking lot has 24 parking spots side by side. What is the width of the parking lot measured in yards?

5   An egg weighs 5 ounces. Ms. Brown uses 4 eggs, a pound of flour, 8 ounces of sugar, and 4 ounces of butter to make a cake. What is the total weight of all the ingredients in pounds?

6   Tyler's kite spool had 100 yards of string. He let out 65 feet of string. The kite then rose another 15 yards. What was the length of string left on the spool in feet?

7. There are two trees in a park. The taller tree is 7 feet. The shorter tree is 9 inches taller than half the height of the taller tree. What is the height of the shorter tree in inches?

8. The driveway in front of a blue house is 19 feet long. The driveway in front of a yellow house is 7 yards long. Which house has a longer driveway? How much longer is the driveway in feet?

Extra Practice and Homework
Conversion of Measurements

Activity 4 Length in Metric Units

Answer the question.

1 What is the height of a classroom door?

　　a　2 cm　　　　b　2 m　　　　c　20 cm　　　　d　20 m　　_____

Write each length in centimeters, or meters and centimeters.

2　6 m 96 cm = _____ cm

3　8 m 90 cm = _____ cm

4　9 m 20 cm = _____ cm

5　9 m 2 cm = _____ cm

6　123 cm = _____ m _____ cm

7 390 cm = _____ m _____ cm

8 365 cm = _____ m _____ cm

9 909 cm = _____ m _____ cm

Write each length in meters, or kilometers and meters.

10 5 km 505 m = _____ m

11 8 km 500 m = _____ m

12 8 km 50 m = _____ m

13 9 km 5 m = _____ m

14 2,050 m = _____ km _____ m

15 7,900 m = _____ km _____ m

16 9,090 m = _____ km _____ m

17 9,009 m = _____ km _____ m

Fill in each blank.

18 7 m 70 cm = _____ cm

19 903 cm = _____ m _____ cm

20 5 km 26 m = _____ m

21 3,056 m = _____ km _____ m

Compare each pair of lengths. Write >, <, or =.

22 81 cm ◯ 8 m 1 cm

23 903 m ◯ 9 km 30 m

24 8 km 8 m ◯ 8,008 m

25 6 km 900 m ◯ 6,009 m

Solve. Show your work.

26 Constance drove 17 kilometers 25 meters from her college to her house for the weekend. Her father drove her back to her college the following day Monday. Her father drove a distance of 26,400 meters. Who drove a longer distance?

27 Mr. Martinez wants to fence up his garden. His rectangular garden is 3 meters 10 centimeters long, and 150 centimeters wide. How many meters and centimeters of fencing does he need?

_____ Date: _____

Chapter 5 Extra Practice and Homework
Conversion of Measurements

Activity 5　Mass and Volume in Metric Units

Answer each question.

1 What is the capacity of a can of drink?

　a　1 L　　　　b　330 mL　　　c　1,500 mL　　_____

2 How heavy is your textbook?

　a　1 kg　　　　b　65 g　　　　c　580 g　　　_____

Write each mass in grams.

3 4 kg 740 g = _____ g

4 5 kg 123 g = _____ g

5 3 kg 40 g = _____ g

© 2020 Marshall Cavendish Education Pte Ltd

Write each mass in kilograms and grams.

6 1,890 g = _____ kg _____ g

7 6,600 g = _____ kg _____ g

8 4,008 g = _____ kg _____ g

Write each volume in milliliters.

9 2 L 450 mL = _____ mL

10 1 L 105 mL = _____ mL

11 6 L 35 mL = _____ mL

12 3 L 9 mL = _____ mL

Write each volume in liters and milliliters.

13 4,900 mL = _____ L _____ mL

14 6,505 mL = _____ L _____ mL

15 2,090 mL = _____ L _____ mL

16 3,005 mL = _____ L _____ mL

Compare each pair of masses. Write >, <, or =.

17 8 kg 69 g ( ) 8,690 g

18 5 kg 250 g ( ) 5,025 g

Compare each pair of volumes. Write >, <, or =.

19 7,600 mL ( ) 7 L 6 mL

20 9 L 99 mL ( ) 9,099 mL

Solve. Show your work.

21 The mass of the turkey that Ms. Wood bought for Thanksgiving last year was 7 kilograms 450 grams. The mass of the turkey she bought this year had a mass of 5,825 grams. Which turkey was heavier? How much heavier was the larger turkey than the smaller turkey?

22 Trinity bought two 2-liter and one 1-liter bottles of juice. She wants to make sure she has enough juice so that she and her 10 friends can each have at least 2 glasses of juice. The capacity of each glass is 240 milliliters. Did Trinity buy enough juice?

Chapter 5

Extra Practice and Homework
Conversion of Measurements

Activity 6   Real-World Problems: Metric Units of Measure

Solve. Show your work.

1   An apple has a mass of 150 grams. The mass of a watermelon is 10 times as heavy as the apple.

   a   What is the mass of the watermelon?

   b   What is the difference in mass between the apple and the watermelon?

2   Clara is 1.5 meters tall. Diego is 0.18 meter taller than her, and 0.2 meter shorter than Trevon. What is Trevon's height in centimeters?

3. Mr. Ortiz is building a wind chime. He needs six 20-centimeter pieces, three 30-centimeter pieces, and one 40-centimeter piece of string. What is the total length of string that he needs in meters and centimeters?

4. Farrah embarks on a walking program. She walks 600 meters on the first day. She will increase the distance by 225 meters each day. Find the distance that she will walk on the 18th day of the program in kilometers and meters.

5 Ms. Chavez will be serving mango juice at a party for her class of 26 students. If she serves 250 milliliters of juice to each student, how many liters and milliliters of juice will she need to buy?

6 The capacity of the tank of a lawn mower is 7,000 milliliters. A 35-liter gas can is filled to the brim with gasoline. How many times will Ms. Torres be able to fill the tank of the lawn mower from the gas can?

7. Adam has a mass of 37.5 kilograms. Cole has a mass of 34.56 kilograms. Grace has a mass of 35 kilograms 65 grams. What is their combined mass in kilograms and grams?

8. Manuel has two cats. He feeds each cat 250 grams of dry food each, twice a day. If he buys a 10-kilogram bag of dry food, how many days will the bag last?

Chapter 5

Extra Practice and Homework
Conversion of Measurements

Activity 7   Time

Write each time in seconds.

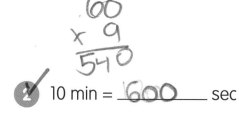

(1) ✓ 9 min = __540__ sec

(2) ✓ 10 min = __600__ sec

(3) ✓ 15 min = __900__ sec

(4) ✓ 3 min = __180__ sec

$$\begin{array}{r} 60 \\ \times 15 \\ \hline 300 \\ 60 \\ \hline 900 \end{array}$$

Fill in each blank.

(5) ✓ 8 min 13 s = __493__ s

(6) ✓ 20 min 47 s = __1,241__ s

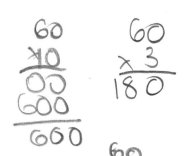

Write each time using the 24-hour clock.

(7) ✓ 6:40 A.M.

__6:40__

(8) 10:05 P.M.

10:05

2205

$$\begin{array}{r} 60 \\ \times 8 \\ \hline 480 \\ + 13 \\ \hline 493 \end{array}$$

$$\begin{array}{r} 60 \\ \times 20 \\ \hline 00 \\ 1200 \\ \hline 1200 \\ + 47 \\ \hline 1,247 \end{array}$$

Write each time using the 12-hour clock.

 0925

$\qquad$ 9:25am $\qquad$

10 2050

$\qquad$ 10:50pm $\qquad$

For each of the following, write down the possible times using the 12-hour and 24-hour clocks.

12-hour clock	24-hour clock
9:30	9:30
9:30	21:30

12

12-hour clock	24-hour clock
3:45	3:45am
3:45	15:45

13

12-hour clock	24-hour clock
12:05	12.05
12:05	00.05

14

12-hour clock	24-hour clock
7:23	7:23
7:23	19:23

Extra Practice and Homework Grade 4B

Answer the question.

15 How long would it take an average swimmer to cover a distance of 100 meters in a competition?

   a 2 min   **b** 2 h   **c** 20 min   _____

Solve. Show your work.

16 A wedding dinner ended at 23 05. The dinner lasted 3 hours 10 minutes. At what time did the dinner start?

17 A soccer match between The Falcons League and Seacrest United lasted 1 hour 45 minutes. The match ended at 18 45. At what time did it start?

18 Zachary arrived at the swimming club at 15 20. He took 42 minutes to travel from his house to the club. At what time did he leave his house?

19 Davi walks from her house to the bus stop every day. She leaves her house at 06 52 and reaches the bus stop at 07 15. How long does Davi take to walk from her house to the bus stop?

20 A movie lasted 2 hours 51 minutes and ended at 00 36 the next day. At what time did the movie start?

21 A New Year party started at 22 30 on Friday. The party ended at 01 15 the next day. How long did the party last?

22 Jordan left her house at 18 00 to go to a musical. She took 50 minutes to reach the theater. She was 10 minutes early. At what time did the musical start?

23 Anna celebrated her birthday on 12 October at 17 45. Her brother celebrated his birthday 18 hours later. Give the date and time of her brother's birthday celebration.

© 2020 Marshall Cavendish Education Pte Ltd

Mathematical Habit 2 Use mathematical reasoning

Luna solved the word problem as follows. Explain what was wrong with her solution.

Word problem:

Hugo ran 3 kilometers 40 meters and Dae ran 680 meters farther than Hugo. Sean ran twice as much as Hugo and Dae. What was the total distance ran by them?

Luna's solution:

Dae's distance = 3 km 40 m + 680 m
              = 340 m + 680 m
              = 1,020 m

Sean's distance = 2 × 1,020 m
                = 2,040 m
                = 2 km 40 m

Total distance = 340 + 1,020 + 2,040
              = 3,400 m
              = 34 km

The total distance ran by them was 34 kilometers.

1 Mathematical Habit **6** Use precise mathematical language

Kevin peeled 3 kilograms of potatoes. His sister peeled 1,900 grams of potatoes.

a Who peeled more? How much more? Give your answer in kilograms and grams.

b Kevin's brother peeled 480 grams less than their sister. How many kilograms of potatoes were peeled in all? Give your answer in kilograms and grams.

2 Mathematical Habit **6** Use precise mathematical language

One dress needs 3 yards of material. Ms. Evans buys a material that is 7 feet 8 inches long. She wants to sew 2 such dresses. How much more material does she need? Give your answer in yards, feet, and inches.

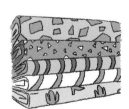

Dear Family,

In this chapter, your child will learn to find the area and perimeter of squares, rectangles, and composite figures, or figures that can be divided into basic figures, such as squares and rectangles. Skills your child will practice include:

- using formulas to calculate the area and perimeter of rectangles and squares
- finding an unknown side of a rectangle or square given its area or perimeter and one known side
- finding the area and perimeter of composite figures
- solving real-world problems involving area and perimeter

Math Practice

Your house and neighborhood offer numerous opportunities for your child to apply his or her knowledge of area and perimeter. At the end of this chapter, you may want to carry out this activity with your child. This activity will help your child reinforce his or her understanding of area and perimeter.

Activity

- Help your child cut and assemble squares and rectangles (ensure that the dimensions are whole numbers) from any kind of paper, to form a composite figure.
  An example of a composite figure is shown.

- Have your child use the squares and rectangles to calculate the area and perimeter of the composite figure.
- Then, discuss with your child other ways to find the area of the composite figure.

Math Talk

Discuss with your child the concepts of **area** and **perimeter** related to rectangles and squares. Have your child talk about how to use formulas for finding area and perimeter.

Explain to your child that a **composite figure** is made up of different shapes. Encourage your child to find the shapes that form the following figures.

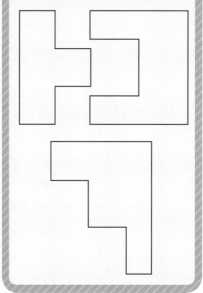

BLANK

Name: _____ Date: _____

Extra Practice and Homework
Area and Perimeter

Activity 1   Area and Unknown Sides

Find the perimeter of each figure.

 1

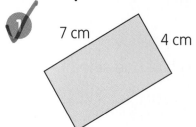

7 cm   4 cm

Perimeter of rectangle

= ___7___ + ___7___ + ___4___ + ___4___

= ___23___ cm

2

6 in.

Perimeter of square = ___6___ × ___4___

= ___24___ in.

Solve. Show your work.

3 The perimeter of a rectangle is 32 yards. Its breadth is 5 yards. Find its length.

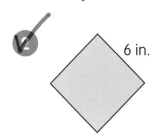

? 11

5 yd   Perimeter = 32 yd   5

11

4 The perimeter of a rectangle is 24 feet. Its length is 9 feet. Find its breadth.

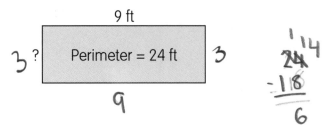

3 ? Perimeter = 24 ft 3

9

$\begin{array}{r} 2\!\!4^{14} \\ -1\,8 \\ \hline 6 \end{array}$

5 The perimeter of a square is 20 meters. Find the length of one side of the square.

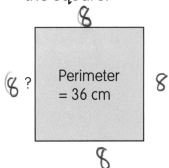

5

5 ? Perimeter = 20 m 5

5

6 The perimeter of a square is 36 centimeters. Find the length of one side of the square.

8

8 ? Perimeter = 36 cm 8

8

Find the area of each figure.

 7

12 cm

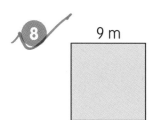

6 cm

Area of rectangle = ___12___ × ___6___

= ___72___ cm²

8

9 m

Area of square = ___1___ × ___4___

= ___36___ m²

Solve. Show your work.

9 The area of a rectangle is 78 square inches. Its breadth is 6 inches.
Find its length.

? 13

Area = 78 in²   6 in.

```
   13
 6⟌78
  −6
   18
```

10 A rectangle has an area of 56 square feet. Its length is 8 feet. Find its breadth.

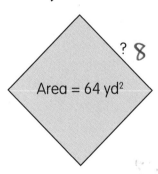

Area = 56 ft² ? 7

8 ft

11 The area of a square is 64 square yards. Find the length of one side of the square.

? 8

Area = 64 yd²

What number when multiplied by itself equals to 64?

$8 \times 8 = 64$

12. The area of a rectangular piece of paper is 48 square inches. Its length is 8 inches.

a. Find its breadth.

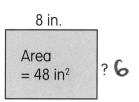

8 in.

Area
= 48 in²

? 6

b. Find the perimeter of the rectangular piece of paper.

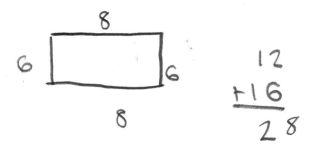

8

6 [ ] 6

8

12
+16
28

13 The area of a square garden is 100 square feet. The length of each side is a whole number.

a Find the length of each side of the garden.

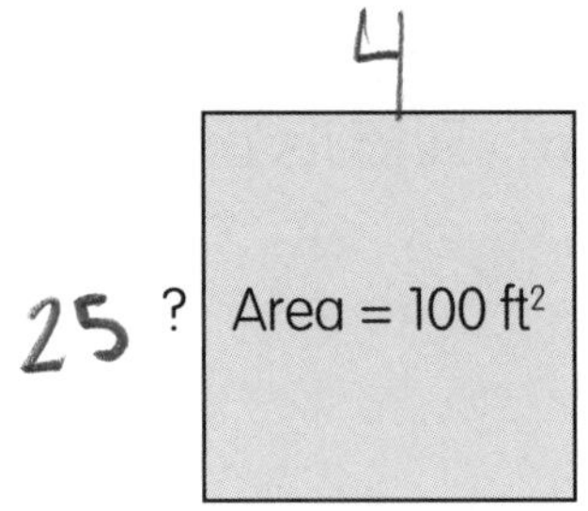

4

25 **?** Area = 100 ft²

b Find the perimeter of the garden.

50
+ 8
———
5 8

25
× 4
———
100

14 The perimeter of a square handkerchief is 28 centimeters.

a   Find the length of each side of the handkerchief.

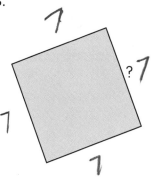

b   Find the area of the handkerchief.

49

15 The perimeter of a rectangular carpet is 48 meters. Its length is 2 meters longer than its breadth.

a   Find its length.

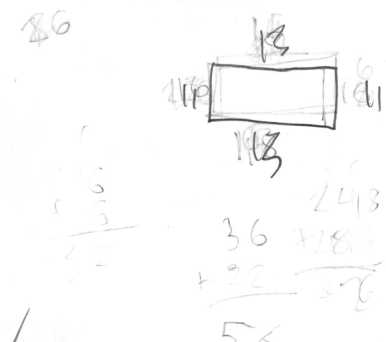

b   Find the area of the rectangular carpet.

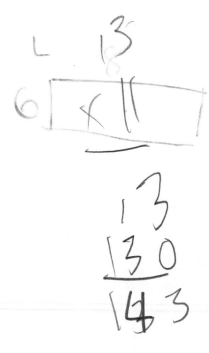

Activity 2   Composite Figures

Find the perimeter of each figure.

1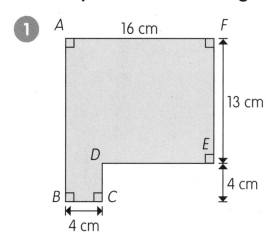

2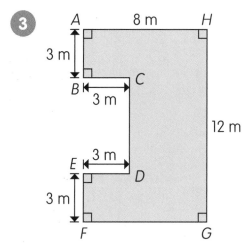

3

4

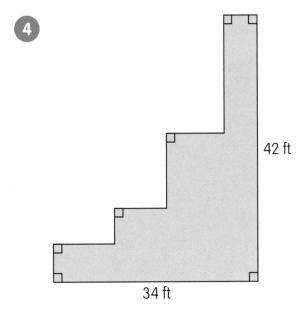

42 ft

34 ft

Find the area of each figure.

5

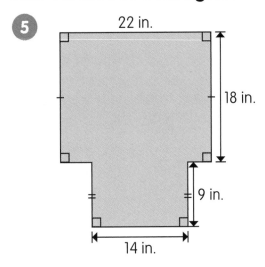

22 in.

18 in.

9 in.

14 in.

6

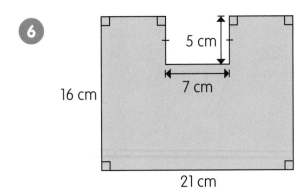

5 cm

7 cm

16 cm

21 cm

7

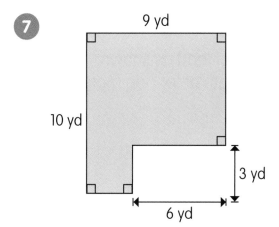

9 yd

10 yd

3 yd

6 yd

8

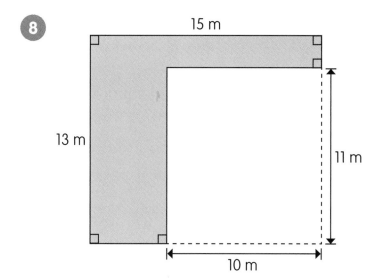

15 m

13 m

11 m

10 m

Solve. Show your work.

9 Xavier wants to put up a fence round the piece of land as shown. Find the perimeter of the piece of land to find the length of fencing material he needs.

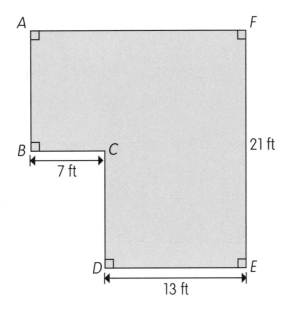

10 A figure made up of two distinct squares has an area of 74 square centimeters. What are the lengths of a side of each square?

Chapter 6 Extra Practice and Homework
Area and Perimeter

Activity 3 Real-World Problems: Area and Perimeter

Fill in each blank.

1 A rectangular field has a rectangular patch of grass removed from one corner. Find the area of the field that is covered with grass.

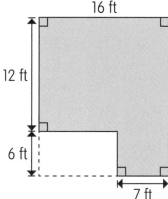

Length of big rectangle = _____ + _____

= _____ ft

Area of big rectangle = _____ × _____

= _____ ft²

Length of unshaded rectangle = _____ − _____

= _____ ft

Area of unshaded rectangle = _____ × _____

= _____ ft²

Area of shaded part = Area of big rectangle − Area of unshaded rectangle

= _____ − _____

= _____ ft²

The area of the field that is covered with grass is _____ square feet.

Solve. Show your work.

2 Amir has a piece of cardboard measuring 90 centimeters by 80 centimeters. She cuts out a small rectangular piece measuring 15 centimeters by 20 centimeters.

a Find the area of the remaining cardboard.

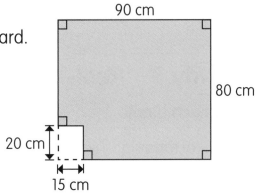

b Find the perimeter of the remaining cardboard.

Use the four-step problem solving method to help you.

3 A carpet is laid on a rectangular floor of length 9 meters and breadth 6 meters. This leaves a margin of width 1 meter round the carpet. Find the area of the carpet.

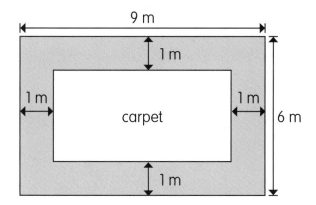

4 A rectangular pond of length 18 yards and breadth 8 yards is surrounded by a path 2 yards wide as shown. Find the area of the path.

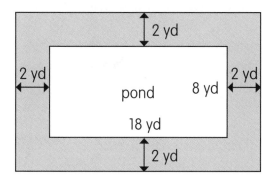

5 A picture is mounted on a frame measuring 25 centimeters by 15 centimeters. It has a border of 3 centimeters round it. Find the area and perimeter of the picture.

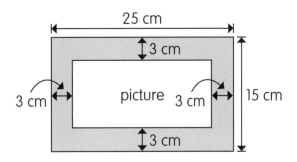

6 Ana makes a path of width 1 meter round her rectangular patch of land. The length and breadth of the outer boundary of the path are shown in the figure. Find the perimeter and area of the rectangular patch of land.

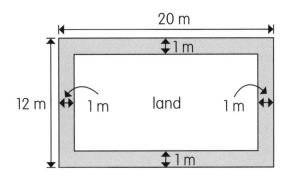

7 The perimeter of the shaded part of a square is 28 inches. Find the area of the square.

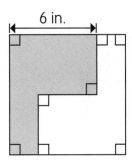

6 in.

8 Two windows each measuring 8 feet by 4 feet are cut out from a wall. The wall has an area of 180 square feet. What is the area of the remaining wall?

9 A rectangular piece of paper is folded to form the figure shown. Find the area of the rectangular piece of paper.

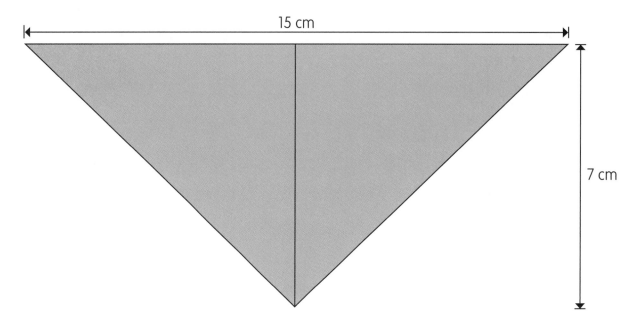

10 A rectangular piece of paper was folded to form the shape shown below. What was the length of the rectangular paper before it was folded?

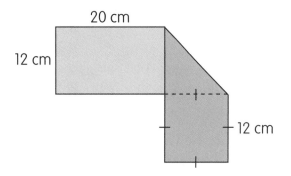

Name: _____ Date: _____

Mathematical Habit 6 | Use precise mathematical language

Which method would you use to find the area of the figure shown?
Explain your choice.

▶ **Method 1**

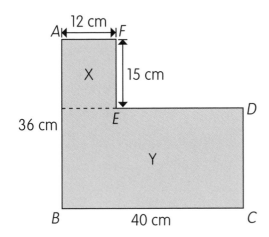

Area of X = 12 × 15
　　　　 = 180 cm²

Length of CD = 36 − 15
　　　　　 = 21 cm

Area of Y = 40 × 21
　　　　 = 840 cm²

Area of figure = 180 + 840
　　　　　　 = 1,020 cm²

▶ **Method 2**

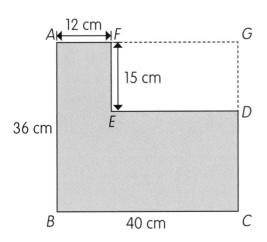

Area of Rectangle ABCG = 40 × 36
　　　　　　　　　　 = 1,440 cm²

Length of DE = 40 − 12
　　　　　 = 28 cm

Area of Rectangle DEFG = 28 × 15
　　　　　　　　　　 = 420 cm²

Area of figure = 1,440 − 420
　　　　　　 = 1,020 cm²

1 **Mathematical Habit 6** Use precise mathematical language

Ms. Lee covers the floor of her living room, which measures 6 meters by 5 meters, with white and grey carpet as shown. Find the area of the floor covered with white carpet.

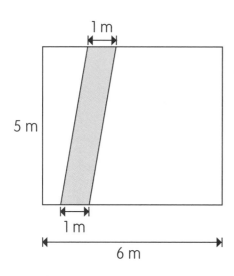

2 **Mathematical Habit 6** Use precise mathematical language

Sara wants to cut 2-centimeter squares from a rectangular piece of paper of length 12 centimeters and breadth 9 centimeters. Find the greatest number of 2-centimeter squares that she can cut from the piece of paper.

SCHOOL-to-HOME
CONNECTIONS

Chapter 7

Angles and Line Segments

Dear Family,

In this chapter, your child will learn about angles. Skills your child will practice include:

- identifying, naming, estimating, and measuring angles
- using a protractor to draw and measure angles
- relating turns to the number of right angles
- understanding what an angle measure of 1° represents
- using addition or subtraction to find unknown angle measures
- solving real-world problems by finding unknown angle measures
- drawing perpendicular and parallel line segments

Math Practice

The study of angles is fundamental to the study of geometry. At the end of this chapter, you may want to carry out this activity with your child. This activity will help to strengthen your child's understanding of angles.

Activity

- Have your child look at the diagram below.

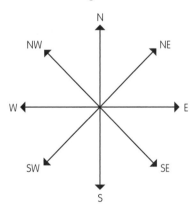

- Ask your child to face a particular direction, for example, north (N).
- Then, ask your child to make a $\frac{3}{4}$-turn clockwise and read the direction he or she is facing (west (W)).
- Continue suggesting $\frac{1}{4}$, $\frac{1}{2}$, and $\frac{3}{4}$ turns, both clockwise and counterclockwise, and having your child read his or her direction after each turn.

 **Math Talk**

Discuss **angles** with your child. Explain to your child that an angle is measured in **degrees**, which is represented by the symbol, °. A **protractor** is used to find the measure of an angle.

Help your child understand:

$\frac{1}{4}$-**turn** is 1 right angle.

$\frac{1}{2}$-turn is 2 right angles.

$\frac{3}{4}$-turn is 3 right angles.

1 full turn is 4 right angles.

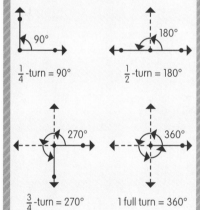

Ask your child to show **clockwise** (same direction as the movement of the hands of a clock) and **counterclockwise** (opposite direction to the movement of the hands of a clock) turns.

BLANK

Chapter **7**

Extra Practice and Homework
Angles and Line Segments

Activity 1   Understanding and Measuring Angles

Name each marked angle.

1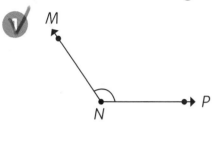

∠ _1125 - MNP_

2 ✓

S

T ___ U

∠ _°90 - STU_

3 ✓

Y

Z

X

∠ _65 - XYZ_

4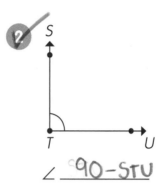

Angle at A = ∠ _25 BAC_

Angle at B = ∠ _118 ABC_

Angle at C = ∠ _42 ACB_

Name each marked angle in another way.

5 ✓

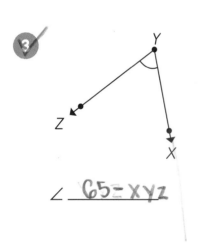

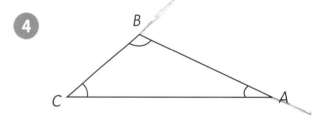

∠p = ∠ _AED_ ✓   ∠q = ∠ _CDE_ ✓

∠BCD = ∠ _DCD_ ✓   ∠BAE = ∠ _EAB_ ✓

Diego is walking along a path. Find the measure of each marked angle along this path.

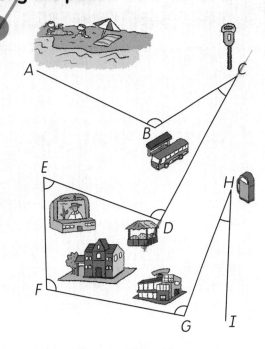

Measure of ∠ABC = ~~125°~~ 124 ✓

Measure of ∠BCD = 30° ✓

Measure of ∠CDE = 100° ✓

Measure of ∠DEF = ~~70°~~ 69 ✓

Measure of ∠EFG = 103° ✓

Measure of ∠FGH = 100° ✓

Measure of ∠GHI = ~~20°~~ 19 ✓

Fill in each blank.

7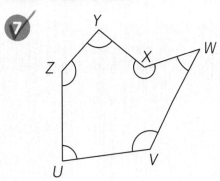

Which marked angles are greater than 90°

in the figure? __UVW, YXW__

8 Measure each marked angle.

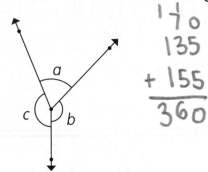

$$\begin{array}{r} 170 \\ 135 \\ +\ 155 \\ \hline 360 \end{array}$$

Measure of ∠a = ~~70°~~ 68 ✓

Measure of ∠b = 135° ✓

Measure of ∠c = ~~155°~~ 157 ✓

What is the sum of the measure of ∠a, ∠b, and ∠c? __360 ✓__

Chapter 7

Extra Practice and Homework
Angles and Line Segments

Activity 2   Drawing Angles to 180°

Use the given protractor to draw an angle with each given angle measure.

1 70°

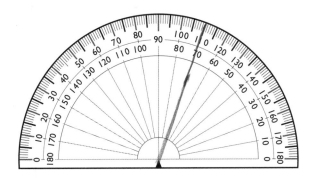

2 147°

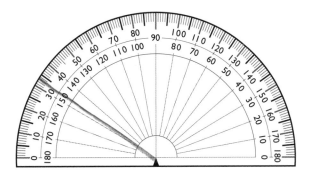

3 108°

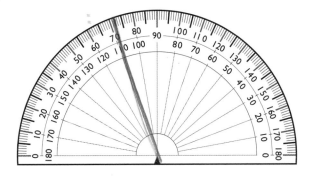

Estimate and join the marked end point of each ray to one of the dots to form an angle with the given measure. Then, measure and label each angle.

4 Measure of ∠p = 105°

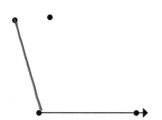

5 Measure of ∠h = 32°

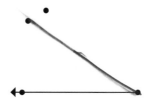

6 Measure of ∠m = 70°

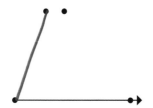

7 Measure of ∠w = 10°

8 Measure of ∠e = 116°

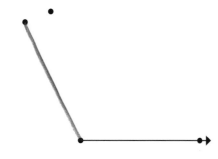

9 Measure of ∠z = 98°

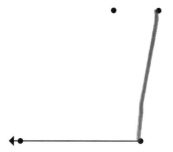

Draw an angle with each given angle measure using the given rays. Then, mark and label each angle.

10   65°

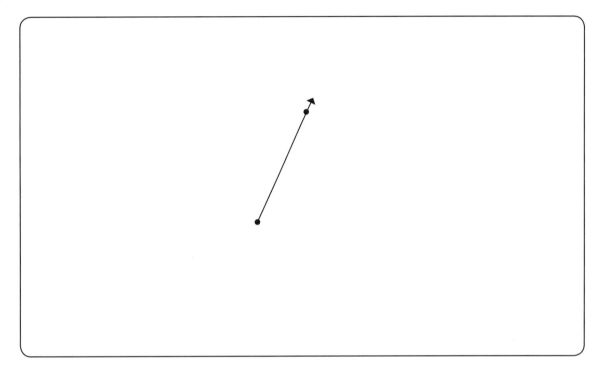

11   162°

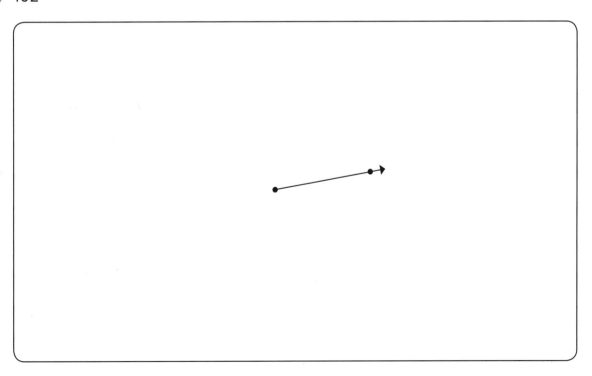

Draw an angle with each given angle measure. Then, mark and label each angle.

12 35°

13 138°

Activity 3   Turns and Angle Measures

Fill in each blank.

 1

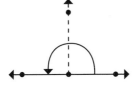

A $\frac{1}{2}$-turn is _____.

2

A _____-turn is 90°.

3

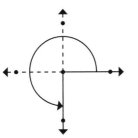

A $\frac{3}{4}$-turn is _____.

4

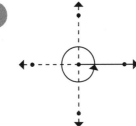

A _____-turn is 360°.

5 Look at each pair of angle strips.

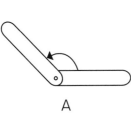

A   B   C   D

Which pair of angle strips shows:

a   a $\frac{1}{4}$-turn? _____   **b**   a $\frac{1}{2}$-turn? _____

c   a turn between a $\frac{1}{2}$-turn and a $\frac{3}{4}$-turn? _____

6 Look at each pair of angle strips.

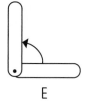 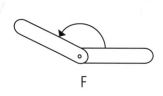 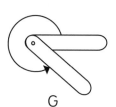 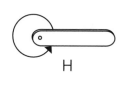

E   F   G   H

Which pair of angle strips shows:

a   90°? _____

b   360°? _____

c   an angle between 180° and 360°? _____

Fill in each blank with the correct fraction.

7 180° makes up _____ of a full turn.

8 Three right angles make up a _____-turn.

9 105° is between a _____-turn and a _____-turn.

Write the measure of each angle.

10 The measure of ∠XYZ is $\frac{5}{8}$ of a full turn.

11 The measure of ∠PQR is $\frac{3}{10}$ of a full turn.

Activity 4 Finding Unknown Angles

Find the measure of each unknown angle.

1 Find the measure of ∠STU.

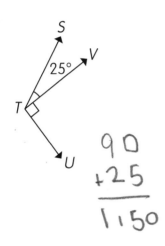

$$
\begin{array}{r}
90 \\
+25 \\
\hline
1150
\end{array}
$$

2 Find the measure of ∠ABC.

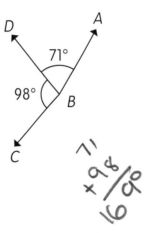

$$
\begin{array}{r}
71 \\
+98 \\
\hline
169
\end{array}
$$

3 Find the measure of ∠XYZ.

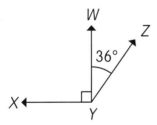

$$
\begin{array}{r}
36 \\
+90 \\
\hline
126°
\end{array}
$$

4 Find the measure of ∠x.

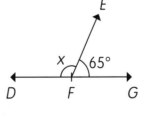

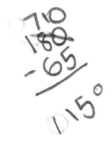

$$
\begin{array}{r}
76 \\
180 \\
-65 \\
\hline
115°
\end{array}
$$

Find the measure of ∠y.

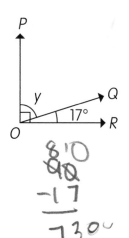

$$\begin{array}{r} 8\,'0 \\ \cancel{9}\cancel{0} \\ -17 \\ \hline 730 \end{array}$$

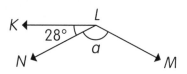 The measure of ∠KLM is 152°. Find the measure of ∠a.

$$\begin{array}{r} 4\,12 \\ 15\cancel{2} \\ -28 \\ \hline 124° \end{array}$$

 A laptop was first opened to a measure of ∠AOB. Then, the measure of the angle was increased by 80°. Find the measure of ∠COB.

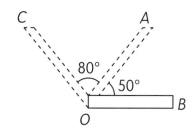

80+50=130

130°

 The clock shows a certain time. Find the measure of ∠z, if the measure of ∠MOP is 135°.

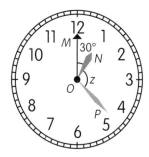

$$\begin{array}{r} 135 \\ -30 \\ \hline 105° \end{array}$$

Chapter 7

Extra Practice and Homework
Angles and Line Segments

Activity 5   Drawing Perpendicular and Parallel Line Segments

For the given line segment, draw a line segment perpendicular to it.

1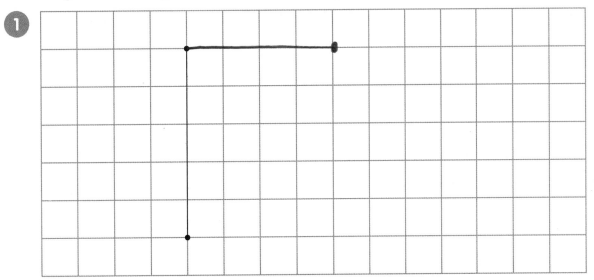

Draw a line segment perpendicular to each given line segment.

2

3

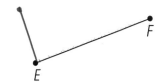

4

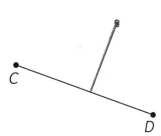

Draw a line segment perpendicular to each given line segment through each given point.

5

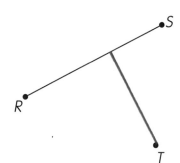

6

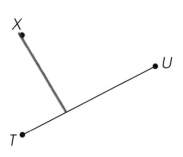

Answer the question.

7 Draw a line segment perpendicular to $\overline{VW}$ through Point *P*. Then, draw another line segment perpendicular to $\overline{VW}$ through Point *Q*.

For the given line segment, draw a line segment parallel to it.

8

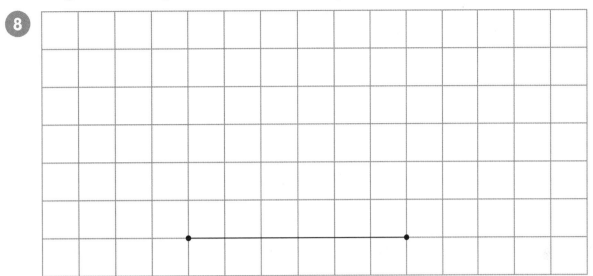

Draw a line segment parallel to the given line segment.

9

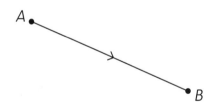

Draw a line segment parallel to each given line segment through each given point.

10

11

Answer the question.

12 Draw a line segment parallel to $\overline{EF}$ through Point T. Then, draw another line segment parallel to $\overline{EF}$ through Point S.

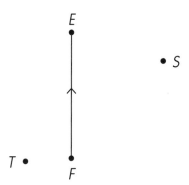

Follow each direction.

13 Draw a line segment perpendicular to $\overline{AB}$ through Point B. Label it $\overline{BC}$.

14 Draw a line segment parallel to $\overline{AB}$ through Point C. Label it $\overline{CD}$.

A •

B •

Answer each question.

15 What is the relationship between $\overline{AB}$ and $\overline{BC}$?

_____

16 What is the relationship between $\overline{AB}$ and $\overline{CD}$?

_____

Extra Practice and Homework Grade 4B

Name: _____ Date: _____

Mathematical Habit 3 **Construct viable arguments**

a   Use a drawing tool on a computer to draw a line segment. Copy and paste the line segment. Are the two line segments parallel? Explain.

_____

_____

_____

_____

_____

b   Draw another line segment. Copy and paste the line segment, select the line segment, and rotate it to make a right angle with the original line segment. Arrange the two line segments so that they meet at one end. Are the two line segments perpendicular? Explain.

_____

_____

_____

_____

_____

1 | Mathematical Habit | **4** | Use mathematical models

Two of the angles in the diagram are 35° each. Name them.

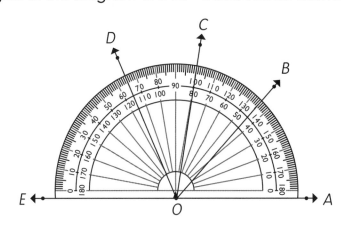

2 | Mathematical Habit | **4** | Use mathematical models

PQ is a lamp post standing vertically. $\overline{RS}$ and $\overline{UT}$ are horizontal line segments on the ground passing through Point Q. $\overline{QT}$ is perpendicular to $\overline{QS}$.

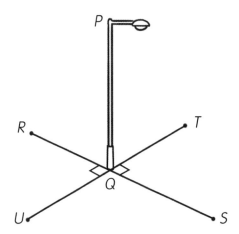

a   Identify two other pairs of line segments that are perpendicular.

_____

b   How many right angles are formed at Point Q? _____

Extra Practice and Homework Grade 4B

SCHOOL-to-HOME CONNECTIONS

Chapter 8

Polygons and Symmetry

Dear Family,

In this chapter, your child will learn more about polygons, and about symmetric shapes. Skills your child will practice include:

- classifying triangles by their angle measures
- classifying quadrilaterals by their properties
- identifying symmetric figures
- identifying and drawing lines of symmetry of figures
- making symmetric shapes or patterns

Math Practice

We are surrounded by symmetry. At the end of this chapter, you may want to carry out these activities with your child. These activities will help to strengthen your child's understanding of symmetry.

Activity 1

- Have your child look at the letters of the alphabet and determine which letters have 0, 1, or 2 lines of symmetry. Look at the following examples together.

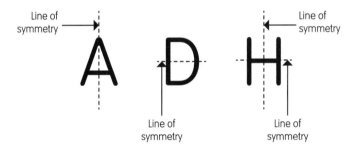

Activity 2

- Go on a symmetry scavenger hunt indoors, outdoors, or both. Indoors, symmetry can be found in eyeglasses, items of clothing, and pet and human faces. Outdoors, symmetry can be found in leaves, butterflies, and street signs.

Math Talk

Encourage your child to talk about **polygons**. A polygon is a closed plane figure formed by three or more line segments. Ask your child to draw examples of polygons, such as squares, and rectangles.

Use the figure below to help your child understand that a **symmetric figure** has at least one **line of symmetry,** and that a line of symmetry is a line that divides a figure into exact halves. The two parts match exactly when folded along the line of symmetry.

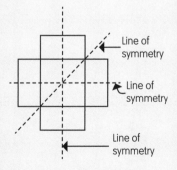

Finally, ask your child to draw lines of symmetry, if any, on the polygons he or she drew earlier. He or she may want to cut out and fold the shapes to check his or her answer.

BLANK

Chapter 8
Extra Practice and Homework
Polygons and Symmetry

Activity 1   Classifying Triangles

Answer each question.

1   Match the triangles to their correct names and descriptions.

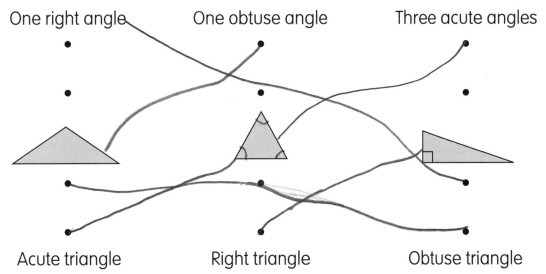

One right angle   One obtuse angle   Three acute angles

Acute triangle   Right triangle   Obtuse triangle

2   Write a description for this triangle.

This triangle is a _____

_____

3   On the dot paper below, draw a triangle that fits this description:
   This triangle has three acute angles.

4 In the figure below, colour
- all the right triangles red,
- all the obtuse triangles yellow, and
- all the acute triangles blue.

You may use a protractor to check the angles.

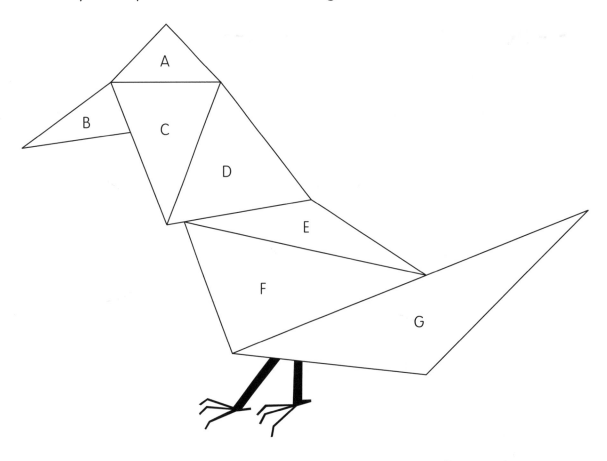

Sort and list the triangles in the figure above.

5 Right triangle: _____

6 Obtuse triangle: _____

7 Acute triangle: _____

Chapter 8

Extra Practice and Homework
Polygons and Symmetry

Activity 2   Classifying Polygons

Fill in each blank.

1 A _____ triangle, a _____, and a _____ each have at least one right angle.

2 A _____ and a _____ have two acute angles and two obtuse angles.

3 A _____ has 1 pair of parallel sides.

4 A _____, a _____, a _____, and a _____ have two pairs of parallel sides.

5 A _____, a _____, and an _____ have only obtuse angles.

Sort the polygons into six groups. Write the letter of each polygon in the correct group. Explain how you have sorted them.

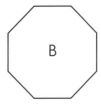
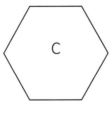
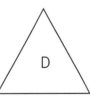
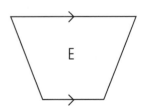

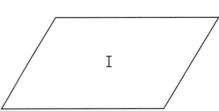

6

At Least One Pair of Parallel Sides	No Parallel Sides

7

At Least One Obtuse Angle	No Obtuse Angles

8

At Least One Right Angle	No Right Angles

Answer the question.

9 Explain why all squares are rectangles but not all rectangles are squares. Draw figures to show your explanation.

Chapter 8

Extra Practice and Homework
Polygons and Symmetry

Activity 3   Symmetric Shapes and Lines of Symmetry

**Circle the letter below each symmetric figure.
Then, draw a line of symmetry for that figure.**

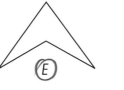

A

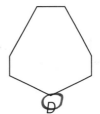

B

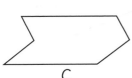

C

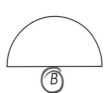

D

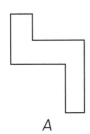

E

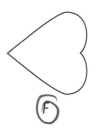

F

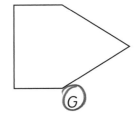

G

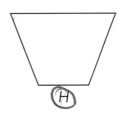

H

Check (✓) the box next to each symmetric figure.
Then, identify the line of symmetry in that figure.

2

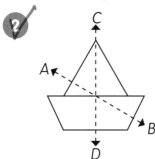

 CD ___

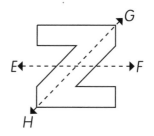

 ~~EF~~ ___

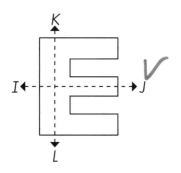 ✓

 IJ ___

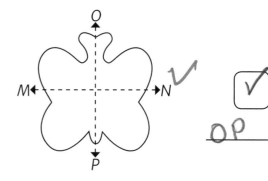 ✓

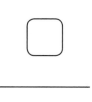 OP ___

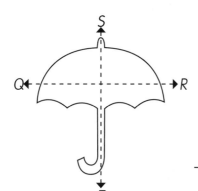

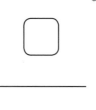 ___

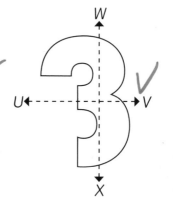 ✓ ✓ ___

Extra Practice and Homework Grade 4B

Is the dotted line in each figure a line of symmetry?
Write "Yes" or "No" in each blank.

3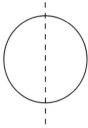

Y ✓

4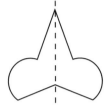

N ✓

5

Y ✓

6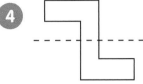

N ✓

7

N ✓

8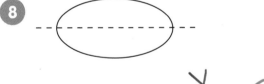

Y ✓

9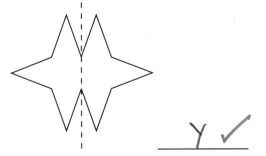

Y ✓

10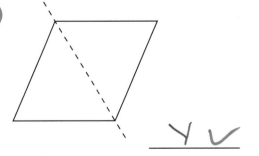

Y ✓

Answer each question.

11 The first United States presidential election was held in 1788. Is the dotted line in each number a line of symmetry? Write "Yes" or "No" in each blank.

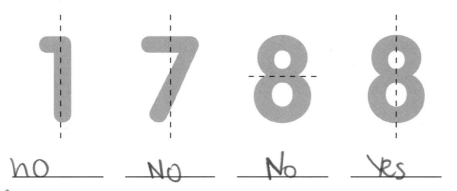

no   No   No   Yes

12 The bald eagle is the mascot of the United States. Is the dotted line in each letter a line of symmetry? Write "Yes" or "No" in each blank.

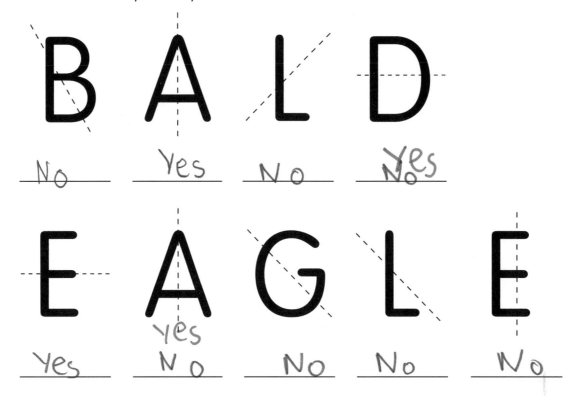

No   Yes   No   Yes

Yes   Yes No   No   No   No

Name: _____ Date: _____

Chapter 8

Extra Practice and Homework
Polygons and Symmetry

Activity 4   Making Symmetric Shapes and Patterns

Complete each symmetric figure with the dotted line as a line of symmetry.

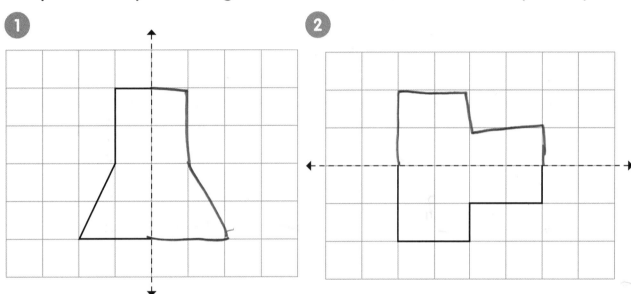

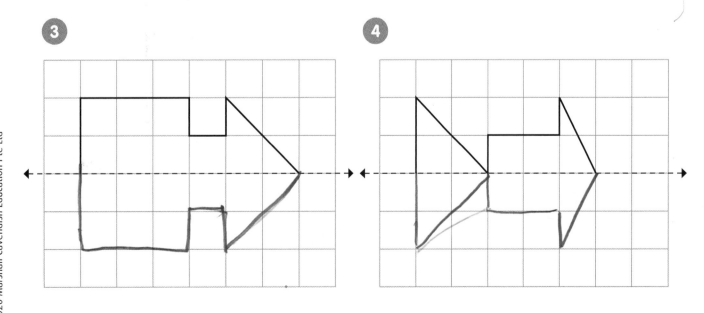

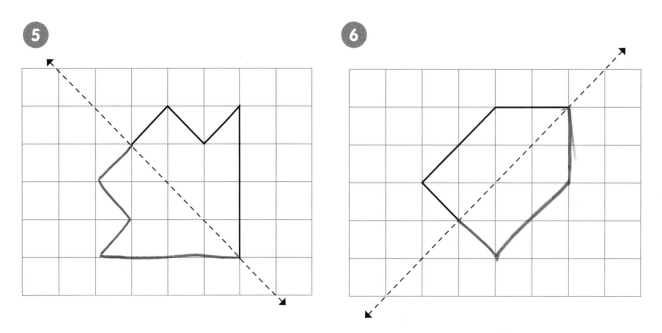

Each figure shows half of a symmetric pattern. The dotted line is a line of symmetry. Shade the squares to form a symmetric pattern about the given line of symmetry.

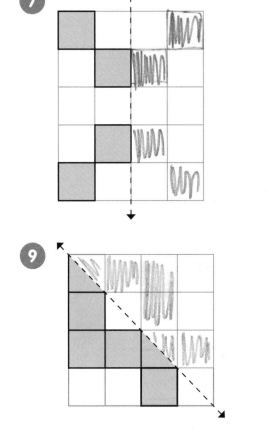

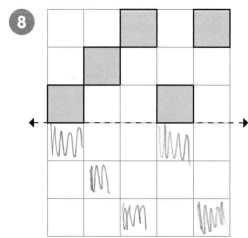

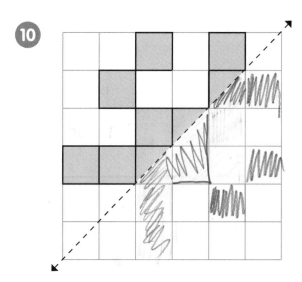

Name: _____ Date: _____

1 **Mathematical Habit 6** **Use precise mathematical language**

Figure *ABCD* is a rectangle.

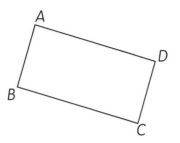

Use the words in the box to fill in each blank.
You may use each word more than once.

opposite	parallel	of equal length
right	sides	four

a   A rectangle has _____ _____.

b   Its _____ sides are _____.

c   Its _____ sides are _____.

d   It has _____ _____ angles.

2 **Mathematical Habit 2** **Use mathematical reasoning**

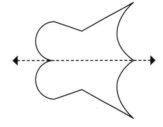

Explain why the dotted line is the line of symmetry for the figure.

_____

_____

Mathematical Habit 5 **Use tools strategically**

Shade whole squares on Grids A and B to create two different symmetric designs. Draw the line of symmetry for each design.

A

B

Chapter 9

Tables and Line Graphs

Dear Family,

In this chapter, your child will learn about tables and line graphs. Skills your child will practice include:

- making and interpreting tables
- interpreting data presented in line graphs

Math Practice

Presenting data, or information in tables and line graphs makes it easier and faster to interpret information. At the end of this chapter, you may want to carry out these activities with your child. These activities will help to strengthen your child's understanding of tables and line graphs.

Activity 1

- Go online to look for pricing tables of some amusement parks.
- Ask your child to interpret how much the tickets for an adult, a child, and a senior cost.

Activity 2

- Go online or look in the newspapers for some line graphs.
- Ask your child to read the axes labels and graph titles, and then describe what each of these graphs represents. Help your child see that line graphs are used to show how data changes over time.

Math Talk

Explain to your child that **data** refers to a set of information and we can collect data using a **tally** chart. A tally mark stands for 1 of something.

The data from the tally chart can be consolidated in the form of a **table** which presents the data in the form of rows and columns.

Help your child understand that a **line graph** shows how data change over time. Together, look for examples of a line graph in your child's math book.

BLANK

Chapter 9

Extra Practice and Homework
Tables and Line Graphs

Activity 1   Making and Interpreting a Table

These are the vehicles that passed through a town center between
10:00 A.M. and 10:15 A.M. last Sunday.

Make tally marks to count the number of each type of vehicle that passed
through the town center.

1 Number of cars   _____

2 Number of motorcycles   _____

3 Number of vans   _____

4 Number of trucks   _____

> Tally marks are used to organize data in groups of 5.

Complete the table using the data in questions **1** to **4**.

5   **Vehicles that Passed Through the Town Center**

Type of Vehicle	Car	Motorcycle	Van	Truck
Number of Vehicles				

© 2020 Marshall Cavendish Education Pte Ltd

The school nurse keeps the health records of nine students. The cards show the height and weight of the students. Use the data on the cards to complete each table.

Name: Alex
Height: 62 in.
Weight: 114 lb

Name: Dae
Height: 59 in.
Weight: 110 lb

Name: Kiara
Height: 55 in.
Weight: 103 lb

Name: Luis
Height: 55 in.
Weight: 114 lb

Name: Lily
Height: 59 in.
Weight: 103 lb

Name: Ella
Height: 62 in.
Weight: 92 lb

Name: Hailey
Height: 55 in.
Weight: 103 lb

Name: Ryan
Height: 51 in.
Weight: 84 lb

Name: Brianna
Height: 55 in.
Weight: 92 lb

6

Height of Students

Height (in.)	Number of Students
51	
	4
	2
62	

Weight of Students

Weight (lb)	Number of Students
84	1
92	
	3
110	
	2

Daniela used tally marks to record the number of pets adopted from an animal shelter in a week.

Pets Adopted from an Animal Shelter

Pet	Tally
Guinea Pigs	卌 ///
Hamsters	卌 卌 卌
White Mice	卌 卌 卌 ///
Rabbits	卌

Use the data in the tally chart to complete the table.

7　　　**Pets Adopted from an Animal Shelter**

Pet	Number of Pets Adopted
Guinea Pigs	
Hamsters	
White Mice	
Rabbits	

Use the data in the table to answer each question.

8　_____ white mice were adopted.

9　_____ guinea pigs were adopted.

10　_____ more white mice than guinea pigs were adopted.

11　Three times as many _____ as _____ were adopted.

12　The pets that were adopted most often from the animal shelter were

_____

Leah has a coin collection. The bar graph shows the number of coins she collected from different countries.

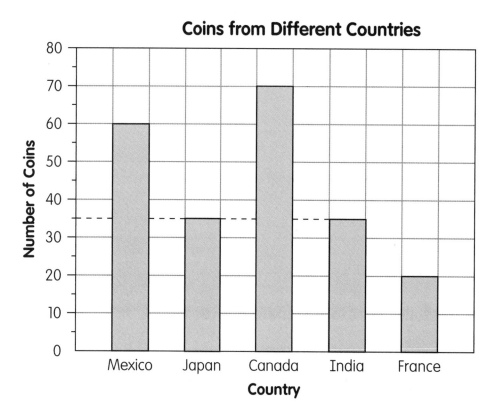

Coins from Different Countries

(Bar graph: y-axis "Number of Coins" from 0 to 80, x-axis "Country")

Mexico: 60, Japan: 35, Canada: 70, India: 35, France: 20

Use the data in the bar graph to complete the table.

13

Coins from Different Countries

Country	Mexico	Japan	Canada	India	France
Number of Coins					

Use the data in the table to answer each question.

14 Leah has half as many coins from Japan as she has from _____.

15 She has _____ more coins from Mexico than from India.

16 The number of coins she collected from _____ is equal to the sum of the number of coins she collected from _____ and _____.

17 The number of Singapore coins that she collected is 25 fewer than the number of coins collected from Canada. She has _____ Singapore coins.

Chapter 9

Extra Practice and Homework
Tables and Line Graphs

Activity 2   Using a Table

Complete each table. Then, answer each question.

The table shows the number of boys and girls in two classes who play and do not play tennis.

1

Students Who Play and Do Not Play Tennis

	Play Tennis	Do Not Play Tennis	Total
Number of Boys	20	16	
Number of Girls		35	49
Total	34		85

2 _____ girls play tennis.

3 _____ students do not play tennis.

4 There are _____ boys in the two classes.

The table shows the number of boys and girls in two classes who wear and do not wear braces.

5

Students Who Wear and Do Not Wear Braces

Class	Number of Girls		Number of Boys		Total
	Wear Braces	Do Not Wear Braces	Wear Braces	Do Not Wear Braces	
4A	10	12	7		42
4B	8		11	12	41

6 _____ students in Class 4B wear braces.

7 _____ girls from both classes do not wear braces.

8 _____ boys from both classes do not wear braces.

The table shows the number of boys and girls going to school by bus or car.

9

Students Going to School by Bus or Car

	Bus	Car	Total
Number of Boys		6	18
Number of Girls	7	17	24
Total	19	23	42

10 _____ boys travel to school by bus.

11 _____ more girls than boys travel by car to school.

12 _____ fewer students take the bus than the car to school.

The table shows the favorite activities of 360 children.

13

Favorite Activities of the Children

Activities	Number of Boys	Number of Girls	Total
Swimming	75	40	
Cycling	53		135
Hiking	31	34	65
Skating		18	45
Total		174	360

14 _____ children like swimming.

15 _____ girls like cycling.

16 _____ boys like skating.

17 There are _____ boys in all.

Extra Practice and Homework
Tables and Line Graphs

Chapter 9

Activity 3 Line Graphs

The line graph shows the temperature recorded over a 12-hour period on a particular day in Hong Kong.

Temperature in Hong Kong on a Particular Day

Use the data in the line graph to answer each question.

1 The temperature recorded at 10 A.M. was _____°C.

2 The highest temperature was recorded at _____.

3 The difference between the highest and the lowest temperatures recorded on the graph was _____°C.

4 The temperature recorded increased by 4°C from _____ to _____.

5 The drop in the temperature recorded was the greatest from _____ to

_____.

Choose a graph to display each data set. Then, explain your choice.

6 A comparison of the number of movie DVDs sold at a shop over five days.

Number of Movie DVDs Sold Over Five Days

Day	Wed	Thu	Fri	Sat	Sun
Number of Movie DVDs Sold	45	55	60	110	100

_____

_____

7 The number of health check-ups a doctor conducted over a six-month period.

Health Check-Ups Conducted Over Six Months

Month	Jan	Feb	Mar	Apr	May	Jun
Number of Health Check-Ups	24	16	52	44	28	40

_____

_____

8 The hours of bike rental over a five-month period by a shop.

Hours of Bike Rental Over Five Months

Month	Mar	Apr	May	Jun	Jul
Number of Hours (h)	1,500	6,000	4,500	2,000	3,500

_____

_____

MATH JOURNAL

Mathematical Habit 6 **Use precise mathematical language**

Coffee Chains A and B provide delivery services. The graphs below show the number of complaints both coffee chains received over four years.

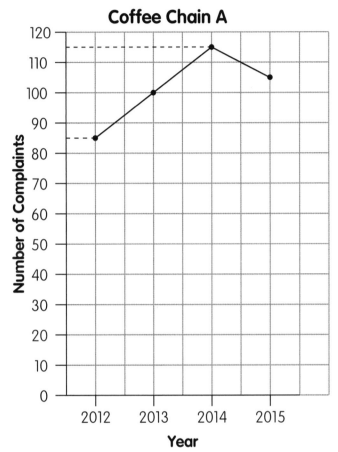

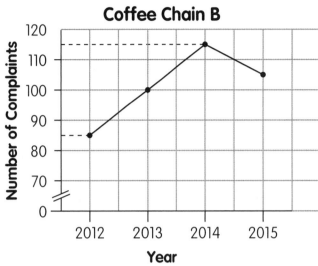

Taylor said that Coffee Chain B received fewer complaints. Do you agree? Explain.

Mathematical Habit 7 Make use of structure

Study the number chart below.

a   Circle the odd numbers. Mark with a cross (✗) the odd numbers which can also be divided exactly by 3. Mark with a tick (✓) the even numbers which can also be divided exactly by 3.

1	2	3	4	5	6	7	8	9	10
11	12	13	14	15	16	17	18	19	20
21	22	23	24	25	26	27	28	29	30
31	32	33	34	35	36	37	38	39	40
41	42	43	44	45	46	47	48	49	50
51	52	53	54	55	56	57	58	59	60
61	62	63	64	65	66	67	68	69	70
71	72	73	74	75	76	77	78	79	80
81	82	83	84	85	86	87	88	89	90
91	92	93	94	95	96	97	98	99	100

b   Then, complete the table to show the data from the number chart.

Type of Numbers	Total
Odd number	
Odd number and can be divided exactly by 3	
Even number	
Even number and can be divided exactly by 3	

c   From the table in **b**, how many numbers can be divided by 6?

_____